NASCAR at the Track

By Mark Stewart & Mike Kennedy

Lerner Publications Company/Minneapolis

The publisher wishes to thank science teachers Amy K. Tilmont and Jeffrey R. Garside of
the Rumson Country Day School in Rumson, New Jersey, for their help in preparing this book.

Lerner Publications Company
A division of Lerner Publishing Group, Inc.
241 First Avenue North
Minneapolis, MN 55401 U.S.A.

Website address: www.lernerbooks.com

All photos provided by Getty Images.

Library of Congress Cataloging-in-Publication Data

Stewart, Mark, 1960-
NASCAR at the track / by Mark Stewart & Mike Kennedy.
p. cm. -- (The science of NASCAR)
Includes index.
ISBN 978-0-8225-8741-5 (lib. bdg. : alk. paper)
1. NASCAR (Association)–Juvenile literature. 2. Stock car racing–Juvenile literature. I. Kennedy,
Mike (Mike William), 1965- II. Title.
GV1029.9.S74S748 2008
796.72–dc22   2007032745

Manufactured in the United States of America
1 2 3 4 5 6 – DP – 13 12 11 10 09 08

Contents

Introduction

From high in the sky, NASCAR tracks look very simple. Most are oval shaped. Areas are set aside for the fans and the racing teams. Of course, a lot more is going on at a track than meets the eye.

This book looks at NASCAR tracks from many different angles. How are they built? Where can fans get the best view? What moves the cars around the track? Why do the cars sound the way they do? The answers to these questions may get you thinking about the world of racing in a whole new way.

THE RACE IS READY TO BEGIN AT THE BRISTOL MOTOR SPEEDWAY IN TENNESSEE. *ABOVE RIGHT:* CARS STREAK PAST FANS AT THE DAYTONA 500 IN FLORIDA.

LEFT: THESE FANS KNEW WHERE TO STAND TO GET AN AUTOGRAPH FROM JIMMIE JOHNSON. BELOW: A NIGHTTIME RACE AT BRISTOL.

Chapter One: From the Ground Up

To be successful, NASCAR drivers must master different kinds of tracks. There are four basic types. A short track is an oval that measures one mile around or less. An intermediate track also has an oval shape. But it is between one and two miles long. A superspeedway is more than two miles from start to finish. Drivers on these oval tracks typically make only left-hand turns. A few races are held on road courses. These are winding tracks with both left-hand and right-hand turns.

No matter how long or what shape a track is, it needs to be designed and built for high-speed driving. This is a job for engineers. Engineers study the science of building. They try to make things as strong and safe as possible. Engineers plan almost everything we see on race day.

CARL EDWARDS WINS A RACE AT THE NASHVILLE SUPERSPEEDWAY IN TENNESSEE. IT IS ONE OF NASCAR'S LONGER TRACKS.

Do the Math

The oval at the Mansfield Motorsports Park in Mansfield, Ohio, is 0.5 mile around. How many laps must drivers complete in a 250-mile race?

(answer on page 48)

TOP: CARS RACE AROUND A TIGHT TURN AT MARTINSVILLE SPEEDWAY IN VIRGINIA. *ABOVE:* FANS GET A GREAT VIEW OF THE ACTION AT THE MANSFIELD MOTORSPORTS PARK IN OHIO. IT IS ONE OF NASCAR'S SHORTEST TRACKS.

Earthmovers

Building a NASCAR track begins by moving dirt. In most cases, more than one million cubic yards of dirt is used. More than 320,000 dump trucks would be needed to move this amount of dirt. Building crews shape the dirt to the plans of the track engineers and architects. A layer of gravel (tiny rocks) is added on top of the dirt. The space between the tiny rocks allows the track to move slightly over time without cracking.

The next step is for the track surface to be poured. Engineers choose which surface material—either concrete or asphalt—to use. They also carefully check the track's grade, or how much the track slopes. They use a special device to make sure the track is shaped correctly from the edge of the infield to the outer wall.

DRIVERS DEPEND ON TRACK BUILDERS TO MAKE RACING SAFE.

HEAVY EARTHMOVERS ARE NEEDED TO BUILD A NASCAR TRACK. *RIGHT:* A HANDHELD DEVICE HELPS TO CHECK THE SLOPE OF THE TRACK.

By Design

The device used to check the grade of a track has a Global Positioning System (GPS). A GPS-guided grader sends a signal to a network of 24 satellites orbiting the earth. The satellites tell the exact position of the device. Engineers use GPS-guided tools to check small measurements on big projects.

On the Surface

The surface of NASCAR tracks is made of either concrete or asphalt. Concrete is made by mixing cement with water and tiny stones. It dries rock hard. Concrete is poured over a framework of steel rods. This makes the surface even stronger. A concrete surface is created in sections, rather than in one circular piece. The sections won't crack when the track gets very hot or very cold.

Asphalt is made of pitch mixed with sand or fine gravel. Pitch is a dark, thick, sticky liquid that is made from crude oil. (Gas for cars also comes from crude oil.) Asphalt tracks are smoother than concrete tracks, which can be bumpy. Most drivers like to race on asphalt because their tires get a better grip on the surface.

THE DIFFERENT TRACK SECTIONS CAN BE SEEN AT
DOVER INTERNATIONAL SPEEDWAY IN DELAWARE.

Do the Math

A fleet of twenty dump trucks is bringing dirt to a NASCAR work site. Each truck can hold 3 cubic yards of dirt at a time. Let's say each truck makes two trips a day. How many cubic yards are coming to the site each day?

(answer on page 48)

SOMETIMES TRACKS ARE DAMAGED DURING A RACE. THIS REPAIR CREW IS WORKING FAST.

In the Mix

When a road surface heats up, it expands slightly. When it gets very cold, the opposite occurs—it contracts (shrinks slightly). Why does this happen? The road surface is made up of atoms (very tiny parts). As the temperature rises, the atoms move faster. They take up more space, so the surface gets bigger. In cold weather, the atoms slow down. They take up less space, so the track gets smaller.

See for Yourself

Over a period of years, the effects of extreme heat and extreme cold can damage a track's surface. To see how atoms react to heat and cold, try this experiment.

- Fill a large bowl halfway to the top with ice-cold water.
- Fill a small soda or juice bottle with very warm water from the sink.
- Empty the bottle, and quickly stretch a small balloon over its mouth.
- Place the bottle in the bowl of cold water. Watch how the balloon is pushed into the bottle.
- Fill another bowl with very warm water. Place the bottle in it. The balloon pops out of the bottle.

A molecule is a group of atoms. An air molecule is made up of two atoms of oxygen. By cooling and heating the air molecules inside the bottle, you can see how the oxygen atoms behave. When a track's surface cools down, the material contracts. This action can cause the track to crack. When the track heats up, the material expands. This action can cause the track to buckle.

The first NASCAR race was held in 1948. Drivers raced on the firm sand of Daytona Beach in Florida. Other tracks were made of dirt. Dirt tracks are still very popular with racing fans.

Shoptalk

"RED CLAY IS THE GREATEST NATURAL RACING SURFACE IN THE WORLD."

—DRIVER CALE YARBOROUGH

A DRIVER WARMS UP HIS CAR DURING A
1940s RACE IN DAYTONA BEACH, FLORIDA.

Chapter Two: Bank on It

A track builder makes a lot of important decisions before building begins. The most important choice is what kind of turns a track will have. Most tracks have an oval shape, with a turn at each end. A few are tri-ovals, meaning there are three big turns instead of two. Each turn is tilted steeply toward the middle of the track.

Why is the track tilted? The answer is speed and safety. When NASCAR drivers enter a turn, they must reduce their speed to keep from going into the wall. A road built at a steep angle helps to change the direction of the car. The greater the angle, the less drivers have to slow down. More speed gets racing fans on their feet!

AT PHOENIX INTERNATIONAL RACEWAY IN ARIZONA, THE TRACK IS SLOPED TO HELP DRIVERS RACE THROUGH THE TURNS.

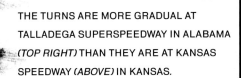

THE TURNS ARE MORE GRADUAL AT TALLADEGA SUPERSPEEDWAY IN ALABAMA *(TOP RIGHT)* THAN THEY ARE AT KANSAS SPEEDWAY *(ABOVE)* IN KANSAS.

Show of Force

The faster an object is moving and the heavier it is, the more the object wants to keep going in a straight line. This is a law of physics called momentum. Physics is the science that explains how bodies in motion behave. Momentum fights against gravity. This is the force that keeps objects on the ground. Momentum also battles with friction. Friction is the grip between the tires and the track that helps a driver to turn a race car.

15

By Degrees

The steepness of turns at a NASCAR track is measured in degrees. Degrees describe the angle formed by two lines. For example, a 90-degree angle looks like the letter L. One-half of that angle would be 45 degrees. The turns at Bristol Motor Speedway in Bristol, Tennessee, are 36 degrees. At Talladega Superspeedway in Talladega, Alabama, the angle is 33 degrees. At the Daytona International Speedway in Florida, the track angles to 31 degrees. Most other tracks have turns banked (sloped) between 10 and 20 degrees.

Tracks such as the Homestead-Miami Speedway in Florida are hardly steep at all. Drivers must be very careful when entering the turns there. One of the fastest tracks in NASCAR is the Texas Motor Speedway in Fort Worth. It has high, long turns and a new racing surface that helps cars hold the road.

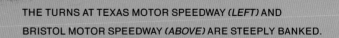

THE TURNS AT TEXAS MOTOR SPEEDWAY (LEFT) AND
BRISTOL MOTOR SPEEDWAY (ABOVE) ARE STEEPLY BANKED.

ABOVE: ON A FAST TRACK LIKE DAYTONA, DRIVERS RACE CLOSE TOGETHER AT VERY HIGH SPEEDS. *BELOW:* FANS GET CLOSE TO THE HIGH-BANKED TURNS AT TALLADEGA.

By Design

A 15-degree angle on a race track may not seem steep. But if you tried to ride your bike up a 15-degree hill, you probably wouldn't make it.

Best Seats in the House

NASCAR fans like to sit where they can see drivers at their best. Fans of Brian Vickers and Denny Hamlin want to watch these drivers race through the turns. Both are very good at judging the forces of speed and momentum. They use this skill to race past other drivers coming out of turns.

Fans of Tony Stewart prefer to sit along the straightaways (straight sections). Stewart goes into turns very fast. Then he slows down rapidly. He often loses ground on the sloped part of the track. He makes up time on the flat, straight sections. At winding road course races, fans roar for drivers like P. J. Jones (right). They are at their best when braking and shifting to take the turns.

Do the Math

Let's say a driver enters a turn at 152 mph and exits the turn at 137 mph. How much speed has the driver lost?

(answer on page 48)

ABOVE: TONY STEWART SPEEDS DOWN THE STRAIGHTAWAY.
BELOW: BRIAN VICKERS (LEFT) DOES HIS BEST RACING IN THE TURNS.

Show of Force

Many drivers are successful because they slow down to go fast. They enter turns slowly to lessen the effects of momentum. This saves wear on their brakes. It also lets them finish turns sooner, so they can go fast again.

See for Yourself

How does a banked turn help cars go faster?
For a better understanding, try this experiment.

- Locate a rubber doorstop, a small block of wood (2 to 3 inches wide), and a spinning tray (also called a lazy Susan).
- Place the wood about halfway between the middle and the edge of the lazy Susan. Start spinning it slowly.
- Increase the speed until the wood slides off the side. At this point, the forces of gravity and friction have lost the battle with momentum.
- Redo the experiment. But this time, place the wood on the doorstop before spinning the tray. The raised end of the doorstop should be pointed outward—like the turn on a NASCAR track.
- Keep increasing the speed until the wood slides off again.

The lazy Susan must spin quite a bit faster before the wood block tumbles off. This is the same idea behind a banked turn.

Too Tough to Tame

One of NASCAR's first great tracks was Darlington Raceway in South Carolina. It was built in 1950. The egg-shaped oval is very challenging. One end of the track has a slightly tighter turn than the other. The two turns are also banked at different angles. If drivers don't pay close attention, they will drift too far to the right and scrape the wall. Racing fans call the streak of paint this leaves the Darlington Stripe.

Shoptalk

"I'D RATHER RUN ON ANY OTHER TRACK THAN DARLINGTON...BUT I'D RATHER WIN AT DARLINGTON THAN ANY OTHER TRACK."

—DRIVER BOBBY ISAAC

DENNY HAMLIN DRIVES CLOSE TO THE WALL AT DARLINGTON. WILL HIS CAR BE THE NEXT ONE TO ADD TO THE DARLINGTON STRIPE?

Chapter Three: Let It Flow

Every NASCAR race involves the use of many liquids. Some liquids—like the beverages the fans drink—you can see. Many more liquids aren't so visible.

A liquid is a substance, such as oil or water, that flows freely. At the track, liquids are used for cooling, heating, and reducing wear on car parts. Of course, the most important liquid at the track is the fuel that powers the cars.

LEFT: J. J. YELEY DOES SOME POWER DRINKING BETWEEN PRACTICE RUNS.

ABOVE: FUEL POWERS CARS, BUT WATER COOLS THEM DOWN ON HOT RACING DAYS.

GREG BIFFLE MAKES A PIT STOP. THE CREW MEMBER AT THE TOP ON THE LEFT IS FILLING BIFFLE'S TANK WITH FUEL.

In the Mix

Racing fuel, like gas for your family's car, comes from crude oil. Crude oil is pumped from deep in the ground and then brought to a refinery. The oil is refined, or changed, into different products, including fuel for NASCAR teams.

Little Bang

Internal combustion engines power the cars at a NASCAR race. In these engines, small, controlled explosions (also called combustions) take place inside the motor. They send power to the wheels, which move the car along the track. What explodes? The combustion is created when a mixture of air and fuel is lit by a spark from a spark plug.

NASCAR fuel is much more powerful than the gas your family buys at a gas station. When the molecules in racing fuel mix with air molecules, they rearrange themselves. The mixture gives off energy in powerful bursts when the spark is added.

MARK MARTIN'S TEAM CAREFULLY DROPS A NEW ENGINE INTO HIS CAR. EVERYTHING MUST FIT PERFECTLY, OR THE CAR WILL LOSE POWER.

In the Mix

Crude oil is a limited resource. One day the earth will run out of it. Will NASCAR teams always rely on the energy supplied by crude oil? If scientists can invent another high-powered fuel, NASCAR will be very interested.

TOP: NASCAR WORKERS EXPLAIN HOW THEY WILL LOOK OVER CARS IN THE FUTURE. *ABOVE:* A MECHANIC TAKES A CLOSER LOOK AT A SPARK PLUG.

Liquid Gold

Motor oil also comes from crude oil. Without motor oil, the metal parts in a race car would heat up and wear out. A thin layer of oil coats engine parts. The oil allows them to move against one another without actually touching.

Another liquid used at NASCAR tracks is hydraulic fluid. It moves energy from one end of a system quickly and smoothly to the other end of a system. Hydraulic fluid operates the steering and brakes on a car. It also powers the jacks used by NASCAR pit crews.

Do the Math

Motor oil comes in one-quart containers. How many containers make up one gallon of motor oil?

(answer on page 48)

HYDRAULIC FLUID POWERS THE JACK THAT RAISES MATT KENSETH'S CAR DURING A PIT STOP.

RIGHT: TO GET THE MOST OUT OF ITS FUEL, A TEAM MAY SWITCH ENGINES BEFORE A RACE. *BELOW:* A CAR'S STEERING ALSO DEPENDS ON FLUIDS.

By Design

The liquid that helps cool NASCAR engines is familiar to everyone—water. A water pump moves water from the radiator, past the engine, where the water takes in heat. The water then circles back to the radiator, where it is cooled before returning to take in more heat.

See for Yourself

How well does water lose the heat it takes in from a car engine? To understand, try this experiment.

- Place a one-cup metal measuring cup in the freezer for 10 minutes. (It's important that the cup is metal, not plastic.)
- Fill two coffee mugs with hot water from the sink.
- Pour one mug of the hot water into the cold measuring cup. Then quickly pour it into a bowl. This is like water returning to a car's radiator.
- Set the bowl and the remaining mug next to each other. Put your finger in each. The temperature in the bowl should be much cooler than the water in the mug.

Water is surprisingly good at drawing heat away from an engine. One of a driver's greatest fears is a broken water pump. Now you know why!

Slick Stuff

The liquid no one wants to see at the track is motor oil from a blown engine. When a motor fails, it sprays oil on the track. Drivers must steer clear of the slick mess. Safety crews must clean it up as quickly as possible. Oil is made to get rid of friction between metal parts. On a track, oil weakens the grip between the tires and the track. So cars can slide when they drive through spilled oil. After hitting an oil spill, a driver can't do much but hope for the best.

Shoptalk

"NO MATTER HOW CAREFUL DRIVERS ARE DURING A RACE, ACCIDENTS HAPPEN."

—DRIVER MARK MARTIN
(ABOVE)

WORKERS CLEAN UP FLUIDS ON THE RACE TRACK DURING A RACE. A FEW DROPS OF OIL CAN CAUSE A CRASH.

Chapter Four: Tough Stuff

The old saying "What you see is what you get" is not always true at a NASCAR race. In fact, a lot of science is behind the many familiar sights at the track. For example, cars and drivers show off a lot of brightly colored materials. These materials often hide real stories of strength and safety. The materials are tough.

Drivers depend on them to stay safe and to win.

SCOTT RIGGS DEPENDS ON HIS CAR AND HIS DRIVING SUIT TO KEEP HIM SAFE.

By Design

Fans often talk about the paint schemes of their favorite cars. But fewer cars are being painted. Many more are being wrapped. In this process, sticky vinyl sheets are applied to the car's body. The sheets are preprinted with the team's colors and the names of its company sponsors.

Bodywork

The outer shell of the cars you see streaking around the track is made almost entirely of sheet metal. Sheet metal is just what it sounds like— metal that has been rolled into thin sheets. It is then pressed into shapes that form the different parts of the car. Sheet metal is good for racing because it is strong and light.

MEMBERS OF KEVIN HARVICK'S CREW WORK QUICKLY TO MAKE A NEW PART FOR HIS CAR.

NASCAR fans will see more carbon fiber material in the years to come. It is already used in several parts of the car, including the rear wing. This is the flat piece of material attached to the back of the car by two small posts. Like sheet metal, carbon fiber material is strong and light.

ABOVE: MECHANICS ATTACH A REAR WING TO A CAR BEFORE THE DAYTONA 500. *LEFT:* KEVIN HARVICK'S CAR IS TOUGH ENOUGH TO RACE WITHOUT A HOOD. *BOTTOM LEFT:* JOE NEMECHECK'S CAR HAS A REAR WING.

By Design

Each strand of carbon fiber is made up of thousands of very light carbon threads. This gives the material great strength. You may own a skateboard or bicycle helmet made with carbon fiber material.

Wheels of Fortune

One of the most common sights at the track is tires. Racing teams use hundreds and hundreds of them! They put a lot of time and money into choosing the right tires. During a NASCAR event, more than 1,000 will be used.

Racing tires are different than the tires on a family car. They don't have the zigzag grooves known as treads. The flat surface of racing tires helps them grip the track. However, they don't work well in the rain. This is why NASCAR officials stop races when the raindrops start falling.

Do the Math

Let's say a racing team tests three different kinds of tires during a practice run. What is the total number of tires they have used?

(answer on page 48)

NASCAR OFFICIALS ARE EVERYWHERE. THEY MAKE SURE THAT DRIVERS USE SAFE TIRES.

DAVID GILLILAND *(LEFT)* LOOKS OVER EVERY INCH OF HIS TIRE AFTER PRACTICE.

In the Mix

Many teams pump their tires with nitrogen gas instead of air. Nitrogen has less moisture in it. So it doesn't expand as much as air on hot days.

A MEMBER OF TONY STEWART'S TEAM KEEPS TRACK OF TIRE INFORMATION ON A COMPUTER.

See for Yourself

Why do treadless tires lose their grip in the rain? Because the tires have no way to channel water away. The moisture forms a thin barrier between the rubber and the road. To see how this happens, try this experiment.

- Cover a pack of gum (or another small, flat object) with a thin coating of plastic wrap.
- Press it down on the bottom of a glass baking dish. Then try to move the pack from side to side.
- The flat, sticky surface of the plastic wrap has formed a tight seal with the glass. This is the same way a treadless tire works with a dry track.
- Cover the bottom of the baking dish with a thin coating of water, and try your object again.
- It's easy to move your pack. In fact, it's almost impossible to make it stay in one place.

This shows you how rain affects treadless tires on a track.

Safety First

Many NASCAR fans wouldn't spot their favorite drivers if they weren't wearing their colorful uniforms. However, these uniforms serve a more important purpose. They protect drivers from the heat of a fire until safety crews arrive. The special material that is used in the uniform linings is also used in helmets and gloves. Drivers know challenges lurk at every turn. That is one of the things they love about racing. But they also know they can depend on their safety equipment.

Shoptalk

"I NEED TO BE WEARING EVERYTHING I CAN WEAR...AND UTILIZE AS MUCH PRECAUTION AS POSSIBLE."

—DRIVER DALE EARNHARDT JR., ON THE IMPORTANCE OF HEAD-TO-TOE SAFETY GEAR

ABOVE: FANS CAN SPOT KEVIN HARVICK *(LEFT)* AND JAMIE MCMURRAY *(RIGHT)* FROM A DISTANCE BECAUSE OF THEIR COLORFUL UNIFORMS. *RIGHT:* DARRELL WALTRIP WALKED AWAY FROM MANY CRASHES, THANKS TO HIS SAFETY EQUIPMENT.

Chapter Five: Fan-tastic!

In most sports, fans are not allowed to watch teams practice. NASCAR fans get to see it all! They can buy tickets for practice runs. This is when teams test their cars before a race. They also pack the track to watch qualifying runs. During qualifying, drivers push their cars as fast as they can to compete for the best starting spots on race day.

THE FANS ARE TREATED TO A FIREWORKS SHOW BEFORE A RACE AT BRISTOL MOTOR SPEEDWAY.

At many NASCAR tracks, racing takes place two weekends a year. Much of the time in between the big events is used to prepare. Track officials must make sure that everything is ready for the drivers and racing teams. They must also be ready to welcome the fans. Most races bring between 50,000 and 175,000 fans to the track.

LEFT: MATT KENSETH ADJUSTS HIS EARPIECE.
BOTTOM LEFT: CASEY MEARS SIGNS AUTOGRAPHS FOR THE FANS AT TRACKSIDE.

Body Language

Fans sitting close to the track often use earplugs. The noise in this area often reaches 130 decibels. Decibels measure sound pressure. Any sound over 100 decibels is very loud.

A Day to Remember

NASCAR fans are great consumers. On race day, they buy a lot of souvenirs. Fans can pick up an official NASCAR T-shirt or cap or necklace almost anywhere. But getting something at the track is extra special. Fans also eat a lot of food and drink a lot of beverages. And every bite or gulp seems to taste a little better. The excitement at a track touches everything in some way.

A FAN HOLDS OUT A SOUVENIR CAR FOR DRIVER
JIMMIE JOHNSON TO SIGN. NASCAR
FANS BUY A LOT OF SOUVENIRS AT RACES.

NASCAR fans are also great consumers of information. At any time—even during a race—they can see where their favorite drivers stand in the Chase for the NASCAR Sprint Cup. This is the yearly NASCAR Sprint Cup Series championship. At the end of each race, drivers are awarded points based on how they finished. These points are added up during the first 26 races. The 12 drivers with the most points then compete for the NASCAR Sprint Cup Series championship in the last 10 races of the year. But even drivers who don't qualify for the Chase still get points based on their finish in each of these final races.

LEFT: A TAILGATING CHEF FIXES DINNER.
RIGHT: CAPS AND SHIRTS ARE BIG SELLERS IN NASCAR STORES AND AT THE TRACKS.

Do the Math

Let's say a track has 20 concession stands. Each sells 1,000 hot dogs during a race. How many hot dogs are sold at the track on race day?

(answer on page 48)

Eyes and Ears

Look around at a NASCAR race, and you will notice that many fans are wearing headphones or earphones. Some are following the race on the radio. Others are using a special scanner to listen in on the chatter between their favorite drivers and crews. This is fun to do during practice and qualifying runs too.

Fans with wireless Internet devices can watch the race in 3-D video. They can follow their favorite cars from three different angles. They can view statistics on the screen. This also is a good way to watch a race on a home computer screen if you can't be at the track.

NASCAR FANS KNOW WHERE TO STAND TO GET A GLIMPSE OF THEIR FAVORITE DRIVERS.

ABOVE: JIMMIE JOHNSON TALKS TO HIS CREW.
RIGHT: A TONY STEWART FAN WATCHES THE ACTION
IN THE GARAGE FROM BEHIND A FENCE. BELOW:
NASCAR OFFICIALS ARE ALSO CONNECTED BY RADIO.

In a Flash

Racing scanners lock on to the two-way radio channels used by drivers and their crews. Before a race begins, fans get a list of channels used by the different teams.

See for Yourself

Race cars make a high-pitched sound as they get near you. They make a low-pitched sound after they pass you. To understand why, try this experiment.

- Switch on a battery-powered toothbrush. Record the sound it makes with a tape player or other recording device.
- Make another recording of the toothbrush in action. But this time, sweep the toothbrush past the microphone, starting and ending about five feet away.
- Listen to the first and second recordings. Notice the difference.

In the second recording, you hear the sound waves being squeezed together as the toothbrush gets closer to the microphone. You then hear the sound waves being pulled apart as the sound waves get farther away. The distance between the waves is also called the frequency.

The Science of Fun

NASCAR is always looking for new ways to make racing more exciting and fun for its fans. Small changes to rules and equipment are made before each season. These are almost always rooted in some branch of science. As you learn the basics of physics, engineering, chemistry, and electronics—and the math behind them—the world of racing will open up in ways you can hardly imagine!

Shoptalk

"RACE FANS ARE THE MOST DEDICATED IN ALL OF SPORTS."

—DRIVER RICHARD PETTY (ABOVE)

KYLE BUSCH THANKS THE CROWD FOR ITS SUPPORT AFTER WINNING A RACE. NASCAR FANS DON'T ALWAYS REALIZE HOW MUCH WORK GOES INTO BUILDING A TRACK AND KEEPING IT SAFE.

Glossary

architect: a person who draws up designs for building projects

atom: the smallest part of a chemical element

consumer: a person who buys or uses a product

cubic yard: a measurement of material such as dirt. A cubic yard of dirt can weigh more than a ton.

degree: a number used to measure angles

friction: the rubbing of one surface against another

grade: the slope of a surface

gravity: the force that attracts things to the center of the earth

hydraulic fluid: a special liquid used in passing energy or force from one place to another

internal combustion engine: the basic engine type for NASCAR race cars

molecule: a group of atoms

momentum: the force or speed an object has when it is moving

NASCAR Sprint Cup Series: the highest level of stock car racing

physics: a branch of science that helps explain movement and energy

pit crew: the seven-member team that takes care of a race car during a race

practice run: a circuit of a race track that helps a racing team test how its car might perform in an actual race

qualifying run: a race for the fastest speed. The fastest qualifiers get spots at the front of the race.

sponsor: the group or person who pays money to support a race or racing team

tire tread: the grooves in a car tire. Tires used in NASCAR races don't have grooves.

Learn More

Books

Buckley, James. *NASCAR*. New York: DK Eyewitness Books, 2005.

Buckley, James. *Speedway Superstars*. Pleasantville, NY: Reader's Digest, 2004.

Doeden, Matt. *Stock Cars*. Minneapolis: Lerner Publications Company, 2007.

Fielden, Greg. *NASCAR Chronicle*. Lincolnwood, IL: Publications International, Ltd., 2003.

Savage, Jeff. *Dale Earnhardt Jr.* Minneapolis: Lerner Publications Company, 2006.

Sporting News. *NASCAR Record & Fact Book*. Charlotte, NC: Sporting News, 2007.

Woods, Bob. *The Greatest Races*. Pleasantville, NY: Reader's Digest, 2004.

Woods, Bob. *NASCAR Pit Pass: Behind the Scenes of NASCAR*. Pleasantville, NY: Reader's Digest, 2005.

Website and Video Game

NASCAR
http://www.nascar.com
NASCAR.com is the official site of NASCAR.
From here you can find information on drivers and their teams, as well as previews of upcoming races, schedules, and a look back at NASCAR's history.

NASCAR 2008. Video game. Redwood City, CA: EA Sports, 2008.
With an ESRB rating of E for "everyone," this game gives fans a chance to experience the speed and thrills of driving in a NASCAR race.

Index

Do the Math Answers

Page 7:   500 laps, 250 laps ÷ 0.5 = 500 laps

Page 10: 120 cubic yards, 3 cubic yards x 2 trips = 6 cubic yards x 20 trucks = 120 cubic yards

Page 18: 15 miles per hour, 152 mph – 137 mph = 15 mph.

Page 26: 4 containers, 4 quarts = 1 gallon, 4 one-quart containers = 1 gallon of motor oil.

Page 34: 12 tires, 3 types tested x 4 tires per test = 12 tires.

Page 41: 20,000 hot dogs, 20 stands x 1,000 hot dogs = 20,000 hot dogs.